Lefka Travel Guide

Sightseeing, Hotel, Restaurant & Shopping Highlights

Angela Woodward

Copyright © 2014, Astute Press
All Rights Reserved.

No part of this publication may be reproduced, stored in a retrieval system, or transmitted, in any form or by any means without the prior written permission of the publisher, nor be otherwise circulated in any form of binding or cover other than that in which it is published and without similar condition being imposed on the subsequent purchaser.

If there are any errors or omissions in copyright acknowledgements the publisher will be pleased to insert the appropriate acknowledgement in any subsequent printing of this publication.

Although we have taken all reasonable care in researching this book we make no warranty about the accuracy or completeness of its content and disclaim all liability arising from its use

Table of Contents

Lefkada 5
    Location & Orientation 6
    Climate & When to Visit 7

Sightseeing Highlights 10
    Lefkada Town 10
    Ducato Cape 10
    Meganisi Island 11
    Nydri Town 12
    Ithaca Island 13
    Egremni Beach 15
    Agia Mavra Castle 16
    Kefalonia Island 17
    Agios Nikitas Village 19
    Porto Katsiki Beach 19
    Vassiliki Town 20
    Skorpios Island 21
    Papanikolis Cave 21

Recommendations for the Budget Traveller 23
    Places to Stay 23
        Geni Garden Apartments 23
        Cosmos Studios 24
        Borsalino Studios 24
        Vliho Bay Hotel 25
        Maistrali Apartments 25
    Places to Eat & Drink 26
        Seaside Restaurant 26
        The Barrel 27
        Stelios Restaurant 27
        JD's Bistro 28
        Mamma Mia 28
    Places to Shop 29
        Nydri Main Street 29
        Vassiliki Main Street 29
        Lefkada Town 30
        Karia Village 30

Land of Lefkas..31

Lefkada

The magical Greek island of Lefkada has been too-often overlooked and tourists and island-hoppers are only now starting to realize what they have been missing. Unaffected by urban Greek life, Lefkada is a holiday paradise with tumbling waterfalls, deep blue oceans and some of the best beaches in Europe.

Western Lefkada is where the best beaches are located and it was decided that this part of the island should not be substantially built upon. Your hotel will most likely be situated on the eastern part of the island with easy daytrips to the beaches. Windsurfing is a popular activity, particularly in the south of the island where there are ideal conditions. Lefkada is a mountainous island and is one of the most popular mountain biking spots in Europe. English is not widely spoken but you'll get by.

The island has been a source of inspiration for many artists from around the world. Some of the most important Greek poets spent time on Lefkada including Aristotelis Valaoritis and Aggelos Sikelianos.

The island was first mentioned in the Greek mythology. It has been inhabited for ages, excavations have found bones from the Neolithic era (around the middle of the 4th millennium BC). Before the union of the Ionian Islands, Lefkada was occupied by the British. In 1864 it inherited by Greece and it has been in the possession of the country ever since. During World War II, Lefkada was occupied by the Italians. After the war ended, the inhabitants focused on expanding the populated areas of the island. It is currently at its all-time peak due to heavy tourism in the last few years.

Location & Orientation

Lefkada is located off the west coast of Greece, and is one of the seven Ionian Islands. It is the fourth largest of that group of islands and the most mountainous. There are three notable towns on the island – Lefkada, Nydri and Vassiliki. Other populated areas are mostly small villages. Most of the tourists that come to the island choose to stay in either Vassiliki or Nydri, with the latter being the most popular resort on Lefkada. One great feature about the island is the fact that it is connected to the mainland Greece with a bridge, so getting in Lefkada is possible by bus or car. There is also an airport just 20 minutes drive away. Although referred to as the Lefkada Airport, its official name is Aktion National Airport. The IATA code of the airport is PVK.

Car Hire companies such as Avis and Europcar offer a variety of vehicles. You can find them in the town of Nydri. If you travel the island by bus, you won't be able to get to as many places as easily as there are four buses daily to most destinations. Less visited attractions are visited by bus twice a day typically. You will find a bus schedule in any tourist information center on the island. A one-way ticket for the bus will cost you €1.60. You can also travel around Lefkada by boat (Trident).

Climate & When to Visit

Summer is the most popular time to visit the island. The peak season is in July and August, with visitors crowding a large portion of the populated areas. Almost all of the activities available in Lefkada are summer activities. The town of Nydri (which is the most popular spot on the island) hardly sleeps during July and August, due to beach parties and nightclubs that are open until the early-hours (such as Sail Inn and Solymar). This is the period when the island is overcrowded with young people and couples, and when you will definitely have a great party time. For today's weather in Lefkada see: http://www.holiday-weather.com/lefkada/

If you want to come mainly to see the natural highlights of the island then any season is good. However, know that a lot of restaurants and shops are usually closed from November to May. If you visit during spring, autumn, or winter you won't find a lot of tourists here. People usually come here for the beach activities.

If you are looking for a more peaceful vacation on Lefkada we suggest you come in June. Although the nightlife is not as active one benefit is that you can access the beach of Porto Katsiki with a boat during this month. This will save you the trouble of having to rent a car to get to one of the most beautiful beaches.

Lefkada has a typical Mediterranean climate, notable for its hot summer and cool winters. The average high temperatures in June are around 32°C. During July and August it gets much hotter, with average high temperatures around 37°C. However, expect to see days when the temperatures go to 40°C. The average low temperature for this season is around 20°C. It can get really hot during this period, but you can always cool off in the lovely Ionian Sea.

The average high temperature during spring is 22°C, while the average low is 11°C. The autumn can get a few degrees hotter. The average high temperature during winter is 11°C and the average low is 6°C.

Sightseeing Highlights

Lefkada Town

The capital city of the island holds the same name as the island. It is located on the northern end of the Lefkada Island. This town has been moving towards a more modern architectural look over the past few years although old houses and structures are still visible throughout Lefkada. The town is pretty calm, so strolling around is pleasant. Be sure to visit the square of Saint Spyridon which is at the center of the town. It is named after the church of Saint Spyridon (built towards the end of the 17th century) which is also located there.

However, the best building in the town is the church of the Evangelistria, otherwise known as the Lefkada Cathedral. You will also find some notable architecture from the 19th century, such as the Town Hall of Lefkada and the Public Library. These buildings were constructed by the British during the period when the island was under their possession.

Ducato Cape

This is a favorite destination for the more adventurous tourists and photographers. Upon getting here, you will be rewarded with views of the islands of Ithaca and Kefalonia. Ducato Cape is at the southernmost destination on the island.

Earlier, the Romans who were betrayed or rejected by the ones they loved were known to jump off this cape. Scuba diving is very popular on this part of the island. There is a sea depth of around 40 meters here and you can see a lot of sea creatures while scuba diving. There are a lot of lobsters here. Note that past diving experience is essential if you want to dive here.

There is a lighthouse located on the territory of the cape. It is situated at the same place where a temple dedicated to Apollo once stood. The lighthouse was built at the beginning of the 20th century. The road to the lighthouse is poor and you will have to drive slowly as there are many rocks that you will encounter on the way. However, once you get there, the scenery will certainly make up for the trouble.

Meganisi Island

Known to the citizens of Lefkada as the Big Island, Meganisi Island is located four nautical miles from Nydri. If you choose to take one of the many daily excursions on the big yachts in Nydri, you will usually stop by Meganisi Island. There are three populated areas on the island, with a total of only 1,500 inhabitants. The island is notable for its caves, with the best known being Papanikolis Cave that you can read about later.

Meganisi is situated southwest of the island of Lefkada, and it will take you about 30 minutes to get to here. This is a really peaceful island with a few beautiful beaches. If you want to spend a few days of your holiday in a really private place, then this island is perfect as it is still pretty much untouched by mass tourism. Meganisi Island is a paradise for couples and the beaches that can be found on Meganisi are secluded. A great thing about the beaches is that they are all within walking distance from the villages. There is a really relaxing atmosphere in every village of the island.

Nydri Town

Nydri represents the most popular tourist destination on the whole island. This town has everything that is needed for a pleasant holiday including a wonderful beach, numerous bars and nightclubs, and plenty of hotels and guesthouses. No matter where you are situated on Lefkada you will most likely go to Nydri at least once.

The popular one-day boat trips to the islands near Lefkada have a starting point at Nydri port. You will see big yachts like Nydri Star and Macedonia Palace that are usually the best choice. A ticket for this one day trip costs around €15 and if you negotiate they may lower the price. These tours will take you around the whole island and to the neighbouring islands. Nydri, much like the rest of the island is perfect for couples and young people. During the night, some parts of the town are very quiet and romantic, while other parts can get live and wild.

A popular activity for tourists staying in Nydri is a visit to Nydri Waterfalls which are located four kilometers from the main street. It is really easy to get to the waterfalls, just follow the signs along the pathway. It is also quite a popular activity to swim in a pond which the waterfall creates. However, be careful, the water is very cold. Once you get back to Nydri, you can relax on the wonderful beach for which the town is known.

Ithaca Island

You shouldn't miss the chance to visit the island of Ithaca and you can reach the island by boat from Vassiliki. These boat transportations are available every day (almost every boat at the Vassiliki harbor will take you here). Ithaca is known for its mention in Homer's Odyssey. Ithaca is well known for its relaxing atmosphere, and people who are visitors to Lefkada sometimes find themselves spending the last few days of their holiday here to relax their mind. The island is known for its peaceful secluded beaches that are usually only accessible by boat.

You will find one town and six villages on Ithaca. Vathi is the biggest area from where you can sail to the above-mentioned secluded beaches. The town has a fairly large harbor that is the center of boat transportation on the island. Two other good locations are the tourist-favorite villages of Kioni and Stavros. Kioni is small but surely makes it up in its beauty and is located in the northern part of Ithaca. Stavros is the second largest populated area on the island of Ithaca and is located in the center of the island.

There are three beaches located on the island that are worth the visit. Two of them are accessible only by boat – Gidaki and Afales.

Gidaki represents the biggest secluded beach on the whole of Ithaca. There is a boat on the harbor of Vathi that will take you to the beach. This boat goes by the name of Gidaki Express. You usually won't find a lot of people here but sometimes groups of tourists visit in August.

Afales may not be the biggest but is one of the most popular beaches on the island. It has perfect white sand and is very peaceful. You will find this beach on the northeastern part of Ithaca.

Kaminia Beach can be accessed by car, but be careful, as the road leading to it is not that great. It is located about 4.5 kilometers from the town of Vathi.

Other than the beaches, there are three notable sites on Ithaca. A favorite site for photographers is the abandoned Pernarakia Monastery. Upon arrival, you will instantly be stunned by the view of all of the Ionian Islands including Lefkada, Meganisi and Kastos.

Upon leaving Vathi and heading towards Stavros you will notice signs for the Kathara Monastery. Follow this road, and you will reach the second notable site on the island. The Kathara Monastery is located 8 kilometers from the town of Vathi and was built in the 18th century. From here you will have a spectacular view of the Vathi bay, which is the third recommended site. More specifically, we recommend that you visit Lazaretto, which is an islet located in the Vathi bay. Several buildings were standing on the islet earlier, but were all destroyed in an earthquake during the second half of the 20th century. However, you will notice that a church is currently standing. You can get there by renting a boat or using the sea taxi services in Vathi.

Egremni Beach

This is the second most popular beach on the whole island of Lefkada (after Porto Katsiki Beach). It is regarded by many as one of the most beautiful beaches in the whole Europe. Egremni Beach is located in the southwestern part of the island, and is really close to Porto Katsiki Beach. The main difference between the two (and the reason why most tourists come to Egremni instead of Porto Katsiki) is the fact that you can access this beach by boat. It is one of the longest beaches on Lefkada at 2.5 kilometers. This helps to avoid overcrowding even during the peak periods of the summer. The ends of the beach are more crowded than the central part, as the latter is mostly for topless or nudist swimmers.

Apart from it being reachable by boat, you can also access Egremni Beach by car. It is highly recommended that you arrive here before 10 in the morning, as you might experience traffic jams later. If you come by car, know that you will have to take 347 steps down to reach the beach. You can find a bar on top of those stairs.

Agia Mavra Castle

You will first have a chance to take a glimpse at this castle while you are arriving on the island, as it is located close to the bridge that connects Lefkada and mainland Greece. The building was constructed in the beginning of the 14th century and was built by the rulers of Sicily, who were then in possession of the island, with the goal to protect it from foes and pirates.

There were several occupations of the territory of Lefkada over the following years, and the castle has been through a lot. Nevertheless, it has been well preserved, much like the rest of the islands treasures. As soon as summer arrives, life is brought back to the castle. There are a few festivals that are organized within the Castle of Agia Mavra. The place is also constantly packed with tourists.

There is a famous church that is located within the complex of the castle. This church was built in the 15th century. The complex once housed administrative structures, as well as quarters dividing the castle. A lot of damage was inflicted on this castle in 1888. Some of the most notable parts of Agia Mavra Castle were destroyed in a fire that year. It was renovated later, and was transformed into a refugee camp. However, that did not last for long, as the Italians had occupied Lefkada, and destroyed parts of the castle with bombs in World War II.

Kefalonia Island

You can visit the Greek island of Kefalonia by boat from Vassiliki, which is available every day. Kefalonia belongs to the group of the seven Ionian Islands. This island is immensely popular for its natural scenery, as well as the clean and friendly villages that can be found all around the island. However, you will have trouble getting to all of these villages because the public bus transportation is not that reliable. You will rarely see island buses in fact. Renting a car is the best decision if you decide to spend more than one day here (there are car hire companies such as Kefalonia RentaCar). Walking to some of the closer destinations is also a good choice.

Argostoli is the main town on the island but is not that popular with tourists. Skala is the town almost all visitors choose to stay and it gets crowded during the months of July and August. It is perfect for a relaxing vacation as it is located next to one of the most popular sandy beaches in the southern part of Kefalonia.

Skala wasn't always situated next to a beach. The old village of Skala was rather located on a hill, and you can still visit this village. It is one of the more popular hiking activities on the island. It will take you about two hours to get there and back.

There are two villages located near Argostoli called Lassi and Leibatho. If you are planning on going on a yacht cruise from Nydri, know that when you make a stop on Kefalonia, you will most likely be visiting the town of Fiskardo (located on the north of the island) and note that this town is a bit pricier than any other on Kefalonia.

There are a few notable beaches on the island. Myrtos Beach is the most famous beach on Kefalonia. During August this northern beach can become really packed with tourists. Note that this beautiful white stone beach is not recommended for kids and non-swimmers as it has an immensely steep shore break.

Another popular beach is Antisamos which is located on the eastern part of the island outside the village of Sami. This beach also becomes crowded during the summers peak.

If you are looking for a more private and peaceful beach, then we suggest you go to Xi Beach. It is located on the western part of the island, south of the village of Lixouri. This beach never seems to attract too many people – we're not sure why though as its one of the loveliest sandy beaches on Kefalonia.

Other than the beach that is located right next to Skala, you would also enjoy Kaminia Beach which you will find near the road when going from the town of Skala to Anno Katelios.

If you want to visit something other than the beaches, then you should know that there aren't too many sites that are worth exploring on Kefalonia. Some sites were destroyed during earthquakes that happened in the past century. There is a notable Roman Villa that is located near Skala where you can see mosaic floors from the Roman era. There are also two caves that are quite the popular tourist attractions – Drogarati and Melissani.

Agios Nikitas Village

This is a really beautiful village that we recommend you visit at least once. A bus from the town of Lefkada goes here and back four times a day. Agios Nikitas is a traditional fishing village, which you will notice right away because of the numerous examples of old architectural styles. These old structures, the wonderful natural surroundings, and the sandy beach make this village one of the most popular spots on the island. The accommodation in Agios Nikitas offers extraordinarily beautiful views. This is one of the reasons why this small village has become more popular recently.

Whether you are staying in this village or just spending a day here, take the time to visit the nearby beach of Kathisma. The distance between these two spots is little less than three kilometers. Kathisma beach is regarded as one of the most beautiful beaches on the island, and is filled with fine, golden sand.

Porto Katsiki Beach

This is one of the most popular sights on Lefkada and is regarded by some as one of the most beautiful beaches in the world. During July and August boats are not allowed to approach the beach so the best way to get here is by car. Note that you will park on a cliff and you will have to go down a lot of steps to get to the beach. If you come to Lefkada in June, then you should have no problem with getting to the beach by boat.

Porto Katsiki Beach is located near the village of Athani. Translated, the name of the beach means Port of the Goat. This name was given because only a goat could reach this area in days gone by. If you come by car you should take a moment to appreciate the view from the parking lot. It is recommended that you arrive here before 10am, since it becomes crowded later.

Vassiliki Town

Vassiliki is the third largest town on the island after Lefkada Town and Nydri. It is located in the southern part of the island and represents the southernmost town of Lefkada. This town is very popular for windsurfers due to its closed bay and the wind that offer great conditions for this sport. Don't worry; even if you didn't bring your gear, there are many shops around the town where you can rent it. Apart from windsurfing, people also enjoy mountain biking here. Sailors are known to be frequent guests in the town. Vassiliki is known for its boat transfers to neighboring islands and almost any boat at the harbor will take you to Ithaca or Kefalonia.

Vassiliki has a beautiful beach and is known its great natural scenery - the whole town is covered in canopy and eucalyptus trees. The road from Vassiliki to the town of Lefkada is 40 kilometers and the road to Nydri is 20 kilometers.

Skorpios Island

Although you will never actually step on this island as it is forbidden to, it is one of the must-sees while on your vacation. You will stop by this island while on a tour with a big yacht like the Nydri Star. Skorpios Island gained fame as the private island of the late Greek billionaire Aristotle Onassis. There are around 200 types of trees here, which were imported from all over the world. The island was controversially sold in April 2013 to the daughter of Dmitry Rybolovlev, a Russian billionaire. Aristotle Onassis had stated that the island should go to the country of Greece if the day came when his family couldn't afford to cover the operating expenses.

Papanikolis Cave

The cave is located in the Island of Meganisi, and you can reach it by boat in 45 minutes from Nydri. If you decide to take a one-day tour with the Nydri Star yacht, you will stop here. It is a significant cave that was once a hideaway for a submarine (called Papanikolis) in World War II. It is a great experience to go into the cave for a swim. Papanikolis Cave is the second largest cave in the whole of Greece.

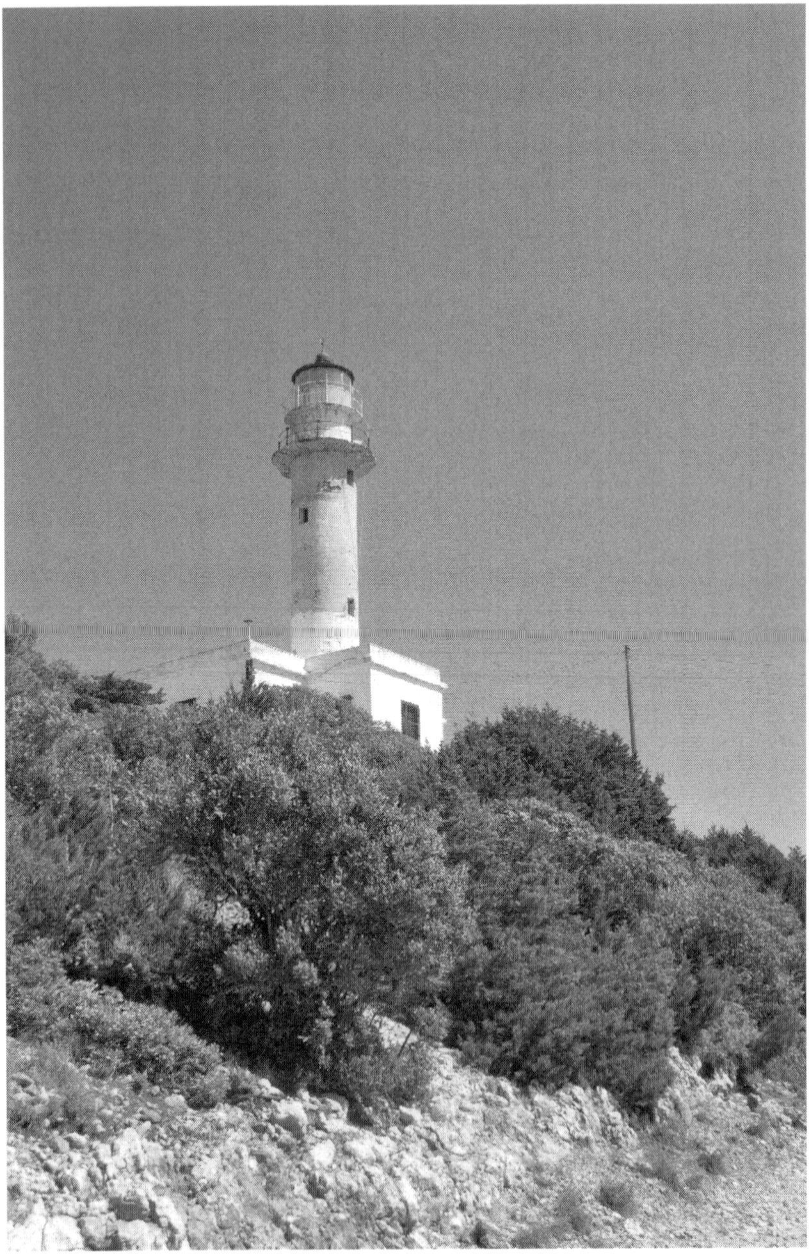

Recommendations for the Budget Traveller

Places to Stay

Geni Garden Apartments

Geni 45
Tel: +30 693 73 89 380

This is one of the best choices when it comes to staying in Lefkada. Geni Garden is located on the Geni Peninsula, within the Vlycho bay. It is situated near the most popular towns on the island – Nydri. This is a perfect spot due to the level of calmness it offers. Apart from it being a very quiet complex, it also offers a great swimming pool. Also, you will see a beautiful flower garden in front of the Geni Garden Apartments that will certainly lure you into spending a relaxing afternoon there. You also have Wi-Fi included in the price of your stay.

This accommodation will cost from €25 per night in June; from €30 per night in July; and from €38 per night in August.

Cosmos Studios

Nydri
Tel: +30 264 50 92 511

This is one of the best places to stay in Nydri. It is close to everything and is only 20 meters from the main street of the town and 80 meters from the beach. The balconies in Cosmos Studios are one of the highlights, as you will find a relaxing atmosphere there. They offer great views of the nature on show in Lefkada. All rooms have a kitchen as well as air conditioning. Note that Wi-Fi is not available in this accommodation. A double room in Cosmos Studios will cost around €60 per night.

Borsalino Studios

Nydri
Tel: +30 264 50 92 528
http://borsalino-studioslefkada.clickhere.gr/

Borsalino Studios is located in the most famous town on the island. It offers some of the finest apartments in the whole town, and they are only 50 meters away from the beach. Unlike some accommodations, Borsalino Studios offers really modern rooms. It is a classy and really quiet place, that won't hurt your wallet too much. Internet access is provided to the guests. A double room will set you back €50 per night in June; €60 per night in July. If you are looking to stay here in August, you will have to contact them to negotiate the price.

Vliho Bay Hotel

Geni
Tel: +30 264 50 95 619
http://www.vlihobay.com/

This is one of the more relaxing hotels that you can find in Lefkada. The staff here is really friendly. It is surrounded with a lot of peaceful nature. Guests of the hotel will also have a pool available for their use. This hotel is located in the village of Geni that is only a few kilometers away from the town of Nydri. It is a quiet village, so you should come here if you plan on spending the nights in a peaceful environment. A double room will set you back €40 per night in June; €60 in the first half of July; and €80 in the other half of July and August.

Maistrali Apartments

Ponti Vassilikis
Tel: +30 264 50 31 039
http://maistrali.weebly.com/

You can find Maistrali Apartments at the outskirts of Vassiliki Town. The rooms are fully equipped and very spacious. Free Wi-Fi is available to the guests. Their balconies offer a beautiful view of the sea. The beach is located only 6 meters away from the apartments. The price for a double room is €55 (per night) in June and the first half of July. In case you are coming in the other half of July, or in August, you will have to pay €75 per night.

Places to Eat & Drink

Seaside Restaurant

Geni
Tel: +30 697 77 35 889
http://www.seaside-lefkada.com/index.php

This is a romantic restaurant but spacious enough for big groups also. Couples can enjoy a meal in the garden overlooking the Vlycho bay. As soon as the night falls, candles are lit that make the ambience even more romantic. It is a family owned restaurant, so know that you will always be properly welcomed.

The whole family is very knowledgeable about the island and tourists often ask them for tips about Lefkada. They offer traditional Greek cuisine, so expect to see a lot of meat on the menu. On another note, their dishes with fresh fish are delightful. This is one of the most popular restaurants on the whole island. However, it is not that expensive. Be prepared to spend around €15-20 for a meal, drink, and dessert.

The Barrel

Nydri
Tel: +30 264 50 92 906
http://www.thebarrel.gr/gb_en.asp

The Barrel is a restaurant that you will find at the harbor of Nydri. It is regarded as one of the best restaurants in the town. They offer both traditional Greek cuisine and international dishes. You will also see a couple of meals that are mixtures of Greek and international cuisine. They also offer a large selection of wines.

The atmosphere is peaceful and the staff is friendly. The restaurant has been open for more than 30 years and is respected by the inhabitants of Nydri. It is pretty cheap - you probably won't spend more than around €15 here.

Stelios Restaurant

Vassiliki
Tel: +30 264 50 31 581

Stelios is a romantic restaurant that you will find by the harbor in the town of Vassiliki. They open only at night, when they are able to provide the perfect atmosphere for a couple. If you are staying in Vassiliki, then you should definitely bring your loved one here. They serve traditional Greek dishes and have an amazing wine selection. Their salads are absolutely delicious.

JD's Bistro

Nydri
Tel: +30 697 03 08 892

You can find JD's Bistro on the main street of the town of Nydri. Unlike most restaurants here, they open long hours – from early in the morning to late at night. This is regarded as the best place to enjoy breakfast on the whole island. Their salads are also highly recommended, and are made from fresh local products. Their menu for the rest of the day is also quite exceptional, and our recommendation would be that you try out their soups. You will have a great meal for around €10 here.

Mamma Mia

Nydri
Tel: +30 264 50 93 102

Mamma Mia is a restaurant that has both longevity and quality. You will find just about everything that you can imagine on their menu. They offer great meat, salads, pastas, and seafood. All of this is prepared in the traditional Greek manner. They are known for their great selection of wine. The restaurant is located by the sea, so expect to have see beautiful views. Mamma Mia is very romantic at night, when they change the atmosphere a bit. During the summer they organize special events, and during this season you can hear live music here. Unlike most restaurants, they work from noon to late at night.

Places to Shop

Nydri Main Street

The main street of Nydri is a pretty long stretch. While strolling along the street you will see a lot of shops. Most of these are selling souvenirs, postcards, and things of that sort. In a few shops you will also find newspapers from all around Europe. Some shops contain interesting handicrafts that were made by certain street artists in the town. There are a few shops located in the town that sell wonderful jewelry with precious stones that are found in the sea. You will also see shops specialized in selling high quality local products. Here you will find exceptional olive oil, cheese, and a large variety of wine.

Vassiliki Main Street

Much like on the main street of Nydri, you can find a lot of shops here. You shouldn't have to worry about souvenirs, as every other shop sells a variety of them. Maybe the most perfect souvenir from Vassiliki would be some of their local produce. Greece is known for their delightful olive oil, which you can find in a few shops here. There are also sell olive oil on the street and it is also of a very high quality.

Lefkada Town

Unlike the towns of Nydri and Vassiliki, you can find some fashion clothing and accessories here. The town of Lefkada has been focusing on opening new stores in the last few years. You can find both local and international clothing brands in this town. You will also see a lot of shops selling locally produced wine. There are some stores that specialize in selling the high quality feta cheese that Greece is known for.

Karia Village

You can find embroidery pieces all across the island of Lefkada. However, if you are looking for the source of all these products, then you should come to the village of Karia. It is a small village located on a mountain and is 14 kilometers from the town of Lefkada. A lot of tourists visit Karia to choose from a wide selection of embroidery work. When you walk into a store, chances are that you will see women making the pieces. They become really busy during the summer.

Land of Lefkas

Tel: +30 264 50 39 139

If you are looking for a place where you can buy some splendid Greek wine, then you should come to the Land of Lefkas. You can find this shop on the road between Nydri and Vassiliki. You will see signs beside the road, so you won't miss the place. It has been opened for more than 10 years, and is pretty well known around the island. They sell a huge variety of locally produced wine.

Printed in Great Britain
by Amazon